BABBLIN' ANIMAL RAPS

WRITTEN BY CHRISTIAN FOLEY

&

ILLUSTRATED BY ROB TURNER

MY NAME'S CHRISTIAN.
A FEW YEARS AGO I HATCHED A PLAN.
I WANTED TO WRITE...

101 RAPS!

(ALL ABOUT ANIMALS)
IT TOOK A WHILE BECAUSE THERE ARE OVER

10,000 WORDS!

RAPS OF MARVELLOUS MAMMALS (THAT RHYME)

1. G-Raf
2. Lion-El Messi
3. A Weird Dessert
4. What Am I?
5. Bouncer
6. Cinderelephant
7. Anti-Establishment
8. The Big Bad Wolf
9. A Terrible Idea
10. Hare Dresser
11. Catnap Rap
12. Sneaky
13. Stop Trying to Make Fetch Happen
14. That's Not a Dog
15. Ringo Dingo Bingo
16. Kangaroo Basketball
17. Can I Know a Rhino?
18. Quokka
19. I am a...

RAPS THAT CLAMBER, CLUTCH AND CLIMB

20. Sturdy McHerdy
21. Grizzly
22. Karla Koala
23. Aye-Aye
24. Lazy
25. Gibbon Rhythm
26. A Lotta Spotted Ocelots
27. Another Terrible Idea
28. Do Chimpanzees?
29. Golden Lion Tamarins
30. Wanna Be
31. Kinkajou
32. Marmot on Toast
33. What If They Had Energy?
34. Flying Squirrels
35. Breakfast
36. 99 Possums

RAPS THAT FLY WITH FLAPPING FEATHERS

37. Duck
38. The Brave Rooster
39. Dough-Dough Dodo
40. If You Don't Like Emus...
41. Deagle the Eagle
42. Goose
43. Show Off
44. Puffin
45. Thief
46. Richie
47. Ray the Ravin' Raven
48. Flamingo DJ
49. An Interesting Audition
50. My Parents are Parrots
51. Owl Vowels
52. Kingfisher
53. Songbird

RAPS WITH SLIMY SKIN, SCALES (OR WHATEVER)

54. Anna Anaconda
55. That's Classic
56. Sprog
57. Hip Hop Frog
58. Cool Punk Skink
59. Gecko
60. Axel Axolotl
61. Armadillo Girdled Lizard
62. The Great British Snake Off
63. At the Car Wash
64. Silly Sally Salamander?
65. Snail Tales
66. Tortoise on Tour
67. Stock Market Croc
68. Isaac Knewton
69. Camille Camille Chameleon

RAPS THAT SCUTTLE, BUZZ, CRAWL OR CREEEEEEP

70. Acro-Bat
71. Centipede Centre Back
72. Yo! Bumblebee
73. Caterpillar Rapper Killer
74. I'm a Celebrity
75. Fight or Flight?
76. Mantras
77. The Nonsense Wasp
78. Shrug
79. Sunday Morning
80. My Grandma's Hairy Ears
81. Cricket
82. Fruit Bat
83. Webster's Words
84. Heads or Tails

RAPS THAT GO SO SO DEEEEEEP

85. Emily Anemone
86. Jellyfish
87. Krill Bill
88. Mobster Lobster
89. Barry
90. Gotta Eat
91. Golfin' Dolphin
92. Skate Fish
93. Dragonfish?
94. Crab Driver
95. Magician
96. Narwhals and Needles
97. Oi Oyster!
98. Shark in the Park
99. A Space in the Sea
100. Dear Humanity
101. I Used to Know an Ocean

RAPS OF MARVELLOUS MAMMALS
(THAT RHYME)

1. **G-Raf**

Raf was a rapper, he had mastered his craft
he practised so much it was actually daft
rapped so many tracks, you would actually laugh
as he bobbled in the bubbles he would rap in the bath

Raf was a rapper, an absolute G
he practised so much that you wouldn't believe
rapped so many tracks, he could rap in his sleep
or when munching on leaves, even brushing his teeth

Raf was a rapper, best rhymer you've known
he practised so much that your mind would be blown
freestyled so well off the top of his dome
that the lions and the leopards always left him alone.

Though Raf was a rapper, there were other rappers too
they gathered in the savannah with their animal crews
there was a rap battle, whose challenging who?
An aardvark said, *"G-Raf what you gonna do!?"*

"I'm G-Raf" he rapped, *"I'm the best, wanna bet?"*
"wanna guess, wanna test? Wanna inspect, check?"
"I'm heads above the rest, better get me respect!"
The rap battle did not finish neck and neck.

2. Lion-el Messi

You can't have a lie in if you want to be the best
I'd be lying if I said this lion lay in for a rest

every morning he'd be training, sunshine or rain
he could make the ball curl like the hairs in his mane

no pausing at all with his paws on the ball
quite short but his awards stacked ten feet tall

trophy after trophy but he hates a trophy hunter
claws like lightning, roar like thunder

his movement, his speed, he does it all so well
plus he dribbles like a lion over meals of gazelle

no lying, no lie ins in if you want to win the title
I'd be lying if I said this lion didn't have a rival

this year no one knows where the award shall go...
Is Lion-el the best or Christiano Prawnaldo?

3. A <u>**Weird Dessert**</u>

We went out for a meal last Wednesday night
the food was good, the vibe was right
the starter was decent, the main was delicious
but after all that, well it all got suspicious...

I ordered dessert; the waiter just sighed
then said, "I'll go fetch him" and went back inside
I thought nothing of it, and continued my wait
while in the kitchen I heard crashing of plates!

The waiter came back, but he wasn't alone
my dessert was with him, I let out a groan
"I won't eat that" I yelled "let him loose!"
That's not what I meant when I ordered A MOOSE!!!

4. <u>What am I?</u>

I fit in your hand

and I point a finger *quick*

I fit in your hand

I zag

and I zig

... and only talk in clicks

5. Bouncer

You ain't comin' in, not tonight lads
dress code is smart casual no trainers...

Are you **MAD!**

You ain't comin' here, not tonight mate
if you wanted in you should have got here

by **EIGHT!!**

I do things by the book
I do things by the letter
my vibe is *'take no bribes'*
well.. unless you've got some feta?
Did you say you had some cheddar?
Some macaroni? Some halloumi?
Still I like a ton of stilton
what you gonna do, *sue me*?

Okay come right in,
this way please, my VIP's
stop a moment for a photo
that's right, *'say CHEESE!'*
I'm the bouncer of the club.
It's basically my house.
I'm the heavy, the enforcer...
I'm the greedy...

DOOR MOUSE!!!

6. Cinderelephant

Cindererelephant Cinderelephant
she did not go to the ball
but that doesn't mean Cinderelephant
was not invited at all.

This story in its elements
is similar to the Disney
Cinderelephant was intelligent
Fairy Godmother, glitzy.

But it's relevant, Cinderelephant
was hungry that night
although evidently elegant
in her dress made by mice

Cindererelephant Cinderelephant
her carriage arrived
Cindererelephant Cinderelephant
ate it all in *ONE BITE!!*

Cinderelephant in her element
was happily munching
she said *"the ball is irrelevant
my favourite food is pumpkin!"*

7. Anti-Establishment

My mother's sisters best beware
if they step anywhere near my lair

my father's sisters better watch their back
next time they bring me round a snack

does your mum have a sister?
I'd love to meet her

does your dad have a sister?
Here's how I'd greet her...

She'd make a great topping for my pizza
that's right I am an... *AUNT EATER!!!*

8. <u>The Big Bad Wolf</u>

The big bad wolf will blow your house down
or chase you around with a terrible frown

this big bad wolf likes leading the pack
she'll have you for dinner for stealing a snack

this big bad wolf will cause you some grief
she'll chomp you right up with removable teeth

she'll howl at you, twirling an old wooden spoon
you'll wish to escape and live on the moon

though this bad wolf isn't always so grumpy
Grandmas not herself whenever she's...

HUNGRY!!!!!!!!!!!!!!!!!

9. A Terrible Idea

What's your worst idea?
I'll take a plunge
my worst idea was a porcupine sponge.

It was a bad idea.
I have to laugh
the time I tried it in the bath...

A terrible idea
I gave up quickly
the sponge was simply way too prickly.

But a better idea
arrived in my head...

How about a porcupine backscratcher instead?

10. Hare Dresser

I'm a hare dresser, that's my job
I've done it most my life
but I get confused when customers
ask for short, back and sides.

I'm a hare dresser, that's my role
I've done this all career
but I get confused when customers
want a shape up for their beard.

They ask for a trim or a clip or a fade
I don't know what to do
I don't have clippers or trimmers or razors
I also have no clue

they look at me funny,
mad hopping like bunnies
all rabbiting on
about wasting their money

then stop for a second, that's when they get it
they suddenly become aware
that I'm not a barber, I help you look sharper

I design clothing for *HARES!!*

11. Catnap Rap

I just meow don't ask me how
better act wowed or this cat goes **POW**

I just meow don't ask me how
better bow down or this cat goes **POW!**

I live like the whole of the street is my house
everyone here I will treat like a mouse

a little bird told me that I am a winner
so I told the bird that I won him for dinner

I just meow don't ask me how
better crowd round or this cat goes **POW!!**

I just meow don't ask me how
crown me now or this cat goes **POW!!!**

I'm the cats pyjamas, an empress perhaps...
I'll destroy all of you right after this nap.

12.   Sneaky

She sprinted so fast
she won every race
when she competed
she'd come in first place

other runners were grumpy
their pride was sore
so they said, *"we'll get her"*
"we'll catch her for sure!"

They all had a meeting
and concocted a plan
to never play fair
whenever she ran

so they'd start to sprint
before the gun said *"go!"*
but she was so focused
that she didn't know!

What a sneaky way
for these sneakies to treat her
and they still had the nerve
to call *her* a cheetah!

13. <u>Stop Trying to Make Fetch Happen</u>

Dodgeball with dogs
we played dodgeball with dogs
we even called it dog-ball.
One team of humans
the other of dogs
we met them in the sports hall.
We had matching kits
they had matching kits
everyone looked the part.
We invited a crowd
and a referee
who blew the whistle to start.

The whistle went
the humans ran
a few yards to get the balls.
But all the dogs stayed
right in their place
did they get the game at all?
We threw the balls
saying "*dodge this dogs*"
but the dogs got us all out.
Everything we threw
they caught in their mouth
before it hit the ground.

Every round was the same
the next and the next
and on the whole game s t r e t c h e d.
We thought the game was dodgeball
but the dogs thought...It was *FETCH*.

14. That's Not a Dog

A dog was just the pet
I'd always wanted to adopt
so when I saw a chance for that
my plan could not be stopped
I saw the advert on a noticeboard
and started looking closer
how was I to know
the truth was missing from the poster

home needed for a dog____
that's all that I saw
so I climbed onto my bicycle
and cycled to the store
the employees at the pet shop
said nothing when I talked
I said "*I can't wait to get my pet
and take her out on walks...*"

They still replied with nothing
to the next thing that I said
that "*this was the type of pet
I'd love to curl up on my bed*"
they brought out a box, I lifted the lid
inside there was something dark
and the box was full of water
in the water was there a shark!?

"*What's happened here!?*" I barked aloud
"*where is my pet and what's this!?*"
I felt lured, I felt tricked
I felt catfished by a dogfish.

15. Ringo Dingo Bingo

Once upon a time
I saw a dingo playing bingo.
He stole the trash can
I said, *"hey where'd the bin go?"*

The dingo was called Ringo
and he squeezed out of the window
lowering his little limbs
like he lumbered up for limbo.

I thought I could describe
what Ringo Dingo did at bingo…
But when I tried to do it
I just didn't have the lingo.

16. Kangaroo Basketball

Gimme that **bounce, dribble, tap**
gimme that **bounce, dribble, tap**
gimme that **clap bam bam bam slap**
when we pass it sounds like that.

Gimme that **bounce, dribble, whoosh**
gimme that **bounce, dribble, whoosh**
gimme that **clap bam bam bam swish**
when we score it sounds like this.

Gimme that **bounce**
gimme that **bounce**
gimme that **bounce**
gimme that **bounce**

BOUNCE
BOUNCE
BOUNCE

that's the KG B'ball sound!

17. Can I Know a Rhino?

How can I know a rhino
when I know they're shy?

So to try know a rhino
should I go say *"hi?"*

And should I show a rhino
my new credit card?

But if I know a rhino

I know that they'll **CHARGE!!**

18. QU**O**KKA

Here is a fact and it might be a *shokka*
here is a fact you can keep in your *lokka*

it might be a fact you learned from *TikTokkas*
nothing on earth likes to eat Quokka!

So they grin and snap selfies, all smiling and cute
so look at a Quokka and you'll feel happy too!

19. I am a...

I'm a magic kind of creature
I'm incredible, I'm rare
my mane remains so precious
like there's silver in my hair

my hoofbeats are like music
my tail whirls with a swish
when I'm trotting in the forest
it's like everything you wished

my eyes are wide with wisdom
my fur shines like it's gleaming
my smile beams, and it might just seem
like right now you are dreaming

but you are not, 'cos this is real
believe in what you see
behold me now before you
and I promise, yes it's me...

I present myself indeed
in my proudest truest form
I'm a magic kind of creature...
I am a...

Horse with an ice cream cone on its head.

20. Sturdy McHerdy

Sturdy McHerdy
was always up early
the sun was still dozing in bed.

But Sturdy was climbing
the starlight was shining
up over the horns in his head.

No harness on back
no rope in his pack
Sturdy just did it alone,

no need for some boots
he had grip on his hooves
this habitat was his home.

To climb is a gift
up the side of a cliff
every crevice he found

He clambered and scampered
a sturdy old dancer
who never ever looked down.

From a high altitude
he admired the view
above where clouds could float...

Sturdy McHerdy
is the best in the world, he
is the mountain *GOAT!*

21. Grizzly

Grant was a grizzly
with no gift of the gab
he grafted and grifted
for fish he could grab

he groaned and he grunted
he grasped and he groped
for his grub in the river
all grimy and gross

Grant was a grizzly
a grumpy old grouch
his grin grew grotesque
gripping fish in his mouth

his grooming was grim
not graceful but grizzled
he gulped down fish soup
and he ground up the gristle

that greasy grey gruel
did not taste so great
but Grant preferred that
to Greek salad and grapes

Grant was a Grizzly
who growled never purred
I once tried to greet him
but he just said...

GRRRRRRRRRRRRRRRR

22. Karla Koala

Karla Koala was sitting in a tree
chewing a bright green tasty leaf
she looked so cute... cuddly... calm
so I held out my hand
and she **CLAWED MY ARM!**

Karla Koala was sitting in a tree
C-H-E-W-I-N-G
she looked so soft with her teddy-bear tum
so I walked right up
but she **BIT MY BUM!**

Now it's hard to be sitting on a seat
I'm C-R-Y-I-N-G
so here is the lesson if you're near her home
and see Karla Koala
just **LEAVE HER ALONE!**

23. Aye-Aye

Would I play eye-spy with an aye-aye?
Aren't their eye-eyes the best in their hood?
Should I play eye-spy with an aye-aye
I... I... don' t think I... I should.

See my eyes are quite like Wi-Fi
I'll try make my line understood
I said my eyes are quite like Wi-Fi
see they don't work in the deep, dark woods.

Would I give Wi-Fi to an aye-aye?
I...I... don't think I... I... could
see staring at the screen in the night-time
wouldn't do their aye-aye eyes any good.

24. Lazy

I'm gonna write a rap
I bet it is the best
but first I'll hang onto this branch
and have a little rest

ZZZZZZZZZzzz

I'm gonna write a rap
it's gonna make the news
but first I'll yawn and stretch a bit
and have a tiny snooze.

Yawwn.

I'm gonna write a rap
I'm gonna diss a moth
but first I'll close my eyes a bit
with all the other sloths.

Yawwwwwwwwwwwn.

I'm gonna write a rap
it'll send the forest crazy
but I bet you'll never hear it
because you're way too lazy!

25. Gibbon Rhythm

I'm a gibbon with a rhythm
better be giving me a ribbon
'cos the rhythm that I'm giving
is a gift.

I'm a gibbon with a rhythm
and I'm driven to deliver
every lyric like its giving you
a lift.

I swing onto the rhythm
and I rip it into ribbons
you could never put a limit
on me...

I'm a gibbon with a rhythm
and I'm living in the middle
of a little bit of brittle
old tree.

26. A Lotta Spotted Ocelots

I lost a lot of ocelots
a lot of them are lost
did you spot a lot of ocelots?
They got a lotta spots.

A lotta spotted ocelots
are glossy in the moss
stalking with velocity
as silently as poss

I found a lot of ocelots
no longer are they lost
stalking with ferocity
and dotted all across.

A lot of spotted ocelots
I spotted that they're cross
they're chasing me
and racing me

I'm gonna pay the cost!

They're chasing me
and tasting me

and showing me who's

BOSS!

27. Another Terrible Idea

He's losing his flock
he's bad at his job
the more that he's lost
the fatter he's got

He just shouldn't do it
he's unqualified
he can't change his spots
(well not that he's tried)

it's easy to count them
you won't fall asleep
for all he has left
is a handful of sheep

their lives are in jeopardy
salted and peppered
this is what you get
when your shepherds a *LEOPARD!*

28. **Do Chimpanzees?**

Do chimpanzees say chimpan-please
when they really wanna chomp on chimpan-cheese?

Do they say bless you when they chimpan-sneeze
into their chimpan-handkerchief?

Do they wanna sail on the chimpan-seas?
Skimming over waves in the chimpan-breeze?

Do they play piano with their chimpan-keys?
Do they laugh at comedies 'til they chimpan-wheeze?

Do they get parking tickets charging chimpan-fees?
Do they put the kettle on for chimpan-teas?

And when they get impressed
and think something is the best

then do they say *"chimpan-jheeeeeeeez!?"*

29. Golden Lion Tamarins

These tamarins are tangerine
and like to play the tambourine
they love to jam at jamborees
and dance until the dawn.

These tamarins are tangerine
and like to scran on cranberries
they love to stamp on trampolines
and bounce until the morn.

These tamarins are tangerine
and like to hear a samba theme
they fill a tank with gasoline
and drive until the night.

These tamarins are tangerine
they're on the go like amber-green
they speed around in limousines
ignoring traffic lights!

30. Wanna Be

I wanna be a wallaby
a wallaby I wanna be
I really wanna wander in the trees

a wallaby I wanna be
I wanna be a wallaby
I really wanna wallow in the leaves

I wanna be a wannabe
a wallaby, a wallaby
I really wanna wallop in the woods

I wanna be a wallaby
a wallaby I wanna be
I waddle and I wobble, *WASSUP!*

31. Kinkajou

Peek-a-boo
I'm a kinkajou
I move just like the ninjas do
I'm too friendly
to injure you
a kinka-who?
a kinkajou.

Peek-a-boo
I'm a kinkajou
I move just like a slinky dude
I'm too shy
I'll slink from you
a kinka-who?
a kinkajou.

Peek-a-boo
I'm a kinkajou
I groove beneath the silver moon
I'm too shy
to wink at you
a kinka-what?
A kinkajou.

Peek-a-boo
I'm a kinkajou
I snooze inside a tree at noon
I'm too shy
I'll hide from you
a kinka-where?
A kinkajou!

32. Marmot on Toast

You hate it or love it
well that's what they say
but how can they do this?
It's just not okay

it's simply just wrong
I don't care about taste
whose idea was it
in the very first place?

You hate it or love it
well that's what they boast
but how can they do this?
Marmot on toast...

Marmot on toast!
MARMOT ON TOAST!

I'll write my MP
I'll protest, I'll vote...

So I wrote my MP
she's just and strong
I said *"do not stop
'til this cruelty is gone"*

the MP wrote back
the reply wasn't long...

I realised that
I had been spelling it wrong.

33. What If They Had Energy?

They're bamboozling amusingly cluelessly snoozing
what are they doing? Nothing, just chewing.

They're bamboozling, confusingly oozing cuteness
how are they doing? No answers they're chewing.

They don't branch out much, just cuddle the trees
they don't ever leave; they just drift off to sleep...

But what if things were different...
What if they had ENERGY!!!!

They could ride Ferris wheels spinning round the fair
they could win some goldfish (in a pair)
they could drive Lamborghinis super-duper quick
they could drift in donuts until they felt sick
they could win the Olympics, stand on the podium...

Then make us pander to all pandas
as they plan more

PANDA-MONIUM

34. Flying Squirrels

Squorville and Squilbur were two squirrel brothers
their second name was Wright.
Squorville and Squilbur
both had a dream
to be capable of flight.

Some squirrels could jump some squirrels could glide
but that's not worth a mention.
Squorville and Squilbur
both had a dream
to fly a plane with an engine.

They scavenged for scraps and cogs and bolts
in their treehouse workshop hut.
Then they added the scraps
and the cogs and the bolts
to their ready-made stash of nuts.

"You're nuts!" said their mum *"you two are nuts*
this is absolutely bonkers!"
"We'll seize the day"
they clapped right back
"you'll come to see we'll conquer!"

Squorville and Squilbur were two squirrel brothers
who knew they would take flight.
Their engine worked
the plane took to the sky
It turned out the brothers were right.

35.<u>Breakfast</u>

I saw a racoon in the back of a spoon
its reflection was

I saw a racoon in the back of a spoon
its expression was

then the racoon leapt over my spoon
its nimble leap was reckless

now all I've got left is just this spoon
because the racoon stole my breakfast!

36. 99 Possums

If you're having pet problems
I feel bad for you son
I've got 99 possums
and I love *EVERY ONE!*

37. Duck

They fly in my space
/
duc**k**
They flock round the place
/
duc**k**
They flap at my face
/
duc**k**

I hate pigeons so very much.

38. The Brave Rooster

He's such a brave rooster
he could fight a T-Rex
with nothing but a toothbrush
sayin' *"who's next!?"*
Wrestle with a werewolf
grapple with a giant
do it with a blindfold
sayin' *"just try it!"*

He could vex vampires
put a hex on a witch
go toe to toe with a tiger
while shaking his fist!
He's such a brave rooster
he could out-sting a scorpion
could even learn to sing
and then perform to an audience

rap in front of strangers
slap a dragon's mouth
have a rave in its cave
with his feet on its couch
He could subdue serpents
battle basilisks
he is such a little star*
just like an asterisk

he's such a brave rooster
he'd give anyone kicking
so why when you see him
do you still call him *CHICKEN!?*

39. Dough-Dough Dodo

Did a dodo use dough-dough
when baking their bread?

Or did a dodo dough-dough
their pizzas instead?

Did a dodo use dough-dough
to dough donuts up?

Or did a dodo dough-dough
some doughballs to dunk?

Did a dodo say *dough!*
when a pastry got burned

Did a dodo say *dough*
for the wages they earned?

Did a dodo earn dough
from the dough-dough they rolled

into donuts and doughballs
and pizzas they sold.

Did dodos even do these baking careers?
I'd ask them but I haven't seen a dodo in years...

40. If You Don't Like Emus...

If you don't like Emus
I think nothing will redeem you.

If you don't like Emus
I'll get lasers and I'll beam you.

If you don't like Emus
I will photograph and meme you.

If you don't like Emus
do you know what I deem you?

If you don't like Emus
I will throw a pie and cream you.

If you don't like Emus
in my nightmares I will dream you.

If you don't like Emus
then my water gun will stream you...

That's what I used to say
until the day I met an...

EMUUUUU_U

41. Deagle the Eagle

Deagle was an Eagle...

If Deagle was kingly
he'd be Deagle the regal Eagle.

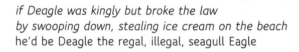

If Deagle was kingly and obeyed the law
he'd be Deagle the regal, legal Eagle

if Deagle was kingly but broke the law
by swooping down, stealing ice cream on the beach
he'd be Deagle the regal, illegal, seagull Eagle

if Deagle was kingly and mostly obeyed
but sometimes broke the law,
by swooping down, stealing ice cream on the beach
then feeding it to a hunting hound...

He'd be Deagle the regal, legal, illegal,
beagle feeding seagull Eagle

plus... If Deagle liked sweet desserts
that made him feel weak,
and he also liked baking
and knitting at the highest point
of a huge church building...

He'd be Deagle the regal, legal, illegal,
beagle feeding, treacle eating, feebly kneading,
seagull Eagle needing a needle on a cathedral steeple.

42. Goose

Flying in formation
cutting through the clouds
scissor sharp wings
slicing high above the ground.

See, he's a fighter pilot
a bird within a plane
G-force at the maximum
Goose can feel the strain.

Hurtling supersonic
screeching through the sky
rocking aviators
yeah, Goose is pretty flyyyyyyy.

He's on a special mission
so he's *speeding* on ahead...

to divebomb
       by the pond
              where there's
                      someone *throwing* bread.

43. Show Off

That peacock is such a show off
he thinks he's in a movie
he's so on fleek, his look's unique
he's all dripped out in *Gucci*

he struts along like all day long
his life's a fashion show
Armani coat, *Versace* tote
his shoes are open toe

his polo shirt is *Ralph Lauren*
he's up on his high horse
his underpants are *Calvin Klein*
and made of silk of course

they all flock to see him
from Cannes up to Milan
his tickets sell out early bird
I heard he's *"BIG IN JAPAN"*

his bed is feathered
his house is a mansion
if you don't think he's handsome
then he'll have a tantrum

why is the peacock like this?
He's such a confident male
how did he become so full of it?
That's a very colourful tail.

44. Puffin

A puffin stole a muffin
and he really wasn't bluffin'
he just opened up a bag
so that he could stuff the stuff in'

the security were huffin'
and they always acted rough in
a bakery where everybody
loved to act so tough in

they caught him but the puffin
then really started bluffin'
he hid away the muffin
and said, *"I didn't do nuffin!"*

45. Thief

She stole my breakfast
she stole my lunch
she stole my sandwich
(which she munched)

she stole my cookie
she took the biscuit
just swooped right in
(and then she nicked it)

she stole my tinsel
she stole my tree
she stole Christmas
(like the Grinch you see)

she stole my wreath
she stole my holly
she stole my presents
(and didn't say sorry)

she stole the night
the snow, the stars
she's famous on
your Christmas cards

I see her thieving
with her head bobbin'
she stole the show
(I call her *Robin*).

46. Richie

Richie the Australian ostrich
was the richest ostrich in Oz,
he afforded ski trips to Austria
and had an ostentatious job

Richie was greatly respected
for his work throughout the land,
every ostrich knew old Rich
even with their head in the sand

Richie was not on osteopath
their job is prodding bodies,
Richie did something similar though
and it was more than a hobby.

His job involved travel
and it kept him on his toes,
every ostrich wanted to run like Rich
'cos Richie was one of the pros

the papers ran stories
he was front page every week,
the news talked about his nose
all the way out in Mozambique

Richie the ostrich was famous
across every nations border,
his job was chasing tourists
and he was top of the pecking order.

47. Ray the Ravin' Raven

Ray the Ravin' Raven
simply radiated rays
with a sunny disposition
he was always wearing shades

Ray would race to raving
whether sunshine or the rain
even if it hailed
that would fail to erase

the joy that Ray could feel
with the volume something mean
if his radio broke
he would rage on that machine

Ray the Ravin' Raven
craved to rave in every field
snacking on a pack of raisins
if he had to raid a meal

Ray was highly rated
for his lovely raving manner
asking the DJ politely...

"Can you play another
BANGER!?"

48. Flamingo DJ

Go flamingo, flamingo go
she spins the records at the flamingo show.

Yo flamingo, flamingo Yo
she mixes tracks like a flamingo pro

Woah flamingo, flamingo woah
she's got one ear in her fly headphones

DJ Flamingo, she's so in sync
dress code for her club...

You must wear pink.

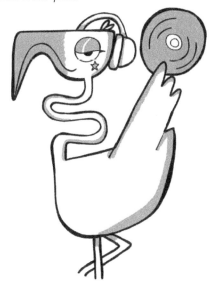

49. An Interesting Audition

The X-factor judges
said the act was so absurd

there were meant to be lyrics
but they couldn't hear a word

if there was some singing
then that would have been preferred

such were the comments
from the judges when they stirred.

Yes the X-factor viewers
thought the act was so absurd

it's a singing competition
but they couldn't hear a word

but I looked at the artist
and made sense of what I heard

she kept her mouth closed
because she was a humming bird.

50. My Parents are Parrots

It is apparent my parents are parrots
they repeat all my poems
and make me eat carrots

Carrots! Carrots! Carrots!

They perch upon my shoulder
and squawk all day
like do they have anything
original to say?

It is transparent my parents are parrots
they repeat all my poems
and make me eat salads

Salads! Salads! Salads!

They perch upon my shoulder
and squawk all night
with their beak in my business
but I guess it's alright
they perch upon my shoulder
but they have my back
even if they do tell me
how I should snack...

It is apparent my parents are parrots!
They repeat all my carrots
and make me eat poems

Poems! Poems! POEMS!

51. Owl Vowels

She doesn't howl, she doesn't growl
nor does she dry herself with towels

she doesn't growl, she doesn't prowl
nor does she get red cards for fowls

she doesn't prowl, but she does scowl
she scowls and scowls and scowls and scowls

she is an owl, an owl, an owl
an owl who only talks in vowels like...

52. Kingfisher

I cast my line, I set my nets
then met what I did not expect

I reeled it in I saw it float
and pulled it in toward my boat

I saw a sword. I saw a shield
and thought, that's not a tasty meal

upon the shield, there was a name
a name that's earned a lot of fame

I gasped for breath; I struggled harder
reeling in our old King Arthur!

A kingfisher I am oh yes
but what I get is never fresh

another king my line has latched
but at this age he's not a catch

53. Songbird

Nina was a songbird
who flew in from the south
where the calming breeze stirred banana leaves
beside the river's mouth.

When she sang
the falling rain fell silent for a beat
it must have stopped to listen
just a moment for a treat.

When she sang
the moon moved nearer with a silver grin
the mists around the mountain swirled
the stars leaned closer in
the oceans waved; the meadows laughed
the trees swayed to the notes
the local fisherman went still
and smiled from their boats
the dawn relaxed; the dusk inhaled
the twilight softly sighed
the three of them felt gentle bliss
listening at each other's side,
the song washed over all the world
it flowed with life like rivers
a voice like ice-cold waterfalls
to chill the spine with shivers.

Nina was a songbird
whose songs enchanted me
and when she sang my heart did too.
In perfect harmony.

54. Anna Anaconda

Anna Anaconda
had a condo
in the amazon
a condo
in the
amazon trees.

Anna Anaconda
had the manners
of an animal
an animal
that didn't
eat leaves.

Anna Anaconda
had an appetite
for anything
for anything
that Anna
ever sees...

and Anna Anaconda
seizes any
opportunity
to greet them
in a
very tight

55. That's Classic

She's very composed
  as she slithers on stage
bows to the audience
  and somehow politely waves

turns to face the orchestra,
  but doesn't raise a hand
the trumpeters begin,
  reading music from a stand

simply with a look,
  she smoothly signals to the strings
the cellos start to bellow
  and here come the violins

the oboes bubble up
  and then the booming double bass,
everybody bobbing heads
  so that they can keep the pace

they watch her at the front
  as she swishes and she sways
either quieting the volume
  or requesting it be raised

after the crescendo,
  everyone is glad they booked her
she's so good at her job,
  she's *the boa-conductor.*

56. <u>Sprog</u>

I'm a tad small
    I'm a tad cold
I'm a tad young
    not a tad old
    in this small **pond**
it's a tad bowl
  I'm a baby **frog**

I'm a
tadpole

57. Hip-Hop Frog

I'm a Hip-Hop frog
on a tip-top log
got swag when I run
that's a Hip-Hop JOG
I'm a Hip-Hop frog
on a tip-top log
writing raps online
that's a Hip-Hop BLOG
I'm a Hip-Hop frog
on a tip-top log
spitting bars in my swamp
that's a Hip-Hop BOG
in a slip-slop bog
on a tip-top log
swapping rhymes with a pug
that's my Hip-Hop DOG
on a tip-top log
in a slip-slop bog
find me rapping in the fog
I'm a Hip-Hop FROG
I'm a Hip-Hop frog
on a tip-top log
rapping to a tadpole

THAT'S MY

HIP-HOP SPROG!

58. Cool Punk Skink

I'm a cool punk skink
all tatted up in ink
my mum says *"it's junk"*
but I don't care what she thinks

I'm a cool punk skink
long eyelashes when I wink
I am really not a monk
I'm a hunk wearing pink

I'm a cool punk skink
feel the funk like I stink
like a skunk that's all dunked
in some gunk as I slink

I'm a cool punk skink
smash guitars in a blink
watch me pulverise pianos
I don't pluck 'em with a plink

I'm a cool punk skink
cans of monster all I drink
always having rock concerts
living underneath your sink!

59. Gecko

I saw a little gecko
and it had a little neck-o,
it was playing cards
it was shuffling the deck-o.

We had a game of chess
and it hit me with a check-o
then we had some porridge
when the gecko wanted brekk-o.

We went scuba diving
and we visited a wreck-o,
I'm kinda scared of swimming
but I figured what the heck-o.

On the shore we found a cave
but I couldn't find the gecko,
so I shouted its name
and I listened to the echo...

GECKO!!!
ECKO!
KO!
ko
°
° °
°
°

60. Axel Axolotl

Axel Axolotl liked to ask a lot of questions
can you answer him
or help me out with some suggestions?

Why is the sky green?
Why is the grass blue?
Why is land watery?
And why do mice moo?

Why do poems rhyme?
But what if they won't?

What if they just wobble around
                the page for no reason
and the words just go EVERYWHERE
and the rhythm disappear.

and what if the poet gets distracted
by their own thoughts
and starts writing about them
instead

like hmmmmm I really liked that yoghurt
I had for breakfast
maybe I'll go to the fridge
and get another one
yeah why not actually.

Why shouldn't I?
I've forgot about Axel Axolotl and his questions
let's just move onto the next page, shall we?

61. Armadillo Girdled Lizard

Some questions...

When the Armadillo Girdled Lizard
goes to sleep
is it a pyjama-dillo Girdled Lizard?

When the Armadillo Girdled Lizard
isn't stressed
is it a calmer-dillo Girdled Lizard?

When the Armadillo Girdled Lizard
acts in a play
is it a drama-dillo Girdled Lizard?

When the Armadillo Girdled Lizard
drives a tractor
is it a farmer-dillo Girdled Lizard?

When the Armadillo Girdled Lizard
tames a snake in the desert
is it a charmer-dillo Girdled Lizard?

When the Armadillo Girdled lizard
makes cheese from a freezing breeze
is it an Armadillo Curdled Blizzard?

When the Armadillo Girdled lizard
jumps over Dumbledore
is it an Armadillo Hurdled Wizard?

I dunno

62. The Great British Snake Off

I could chew blueberry
very yummy when I do
I could chew some cherry
very lovely when its new

I could tuck into some peach
I could snack upon some cream
I could grapple with some apple
apple's actually a dream

I could dunk into some pumpkin
whip up rhubarb just for me
get my jaws into some strawberry
I'm more merry after tea

let me sneak in extra pecan
and some Mississippi Mud
then it rumbles in my stomach
and it tumbles in and it thuds

my appetite is not petite
I slurp up food just like a syphon
I have all of the above
because I'm actually a pie-thon

63. At the Car Wash

We took my Lambo to be cleaned up
at the car wash down the road
it's just by the local pond
and it's owner is a toad.

Some employees there are bullfrogs
there are others who are snakes
but I take my Lambo there
because I can afford the rates.

Snakes slither on the vehicle
sudding soap on all the glass
seven silky serpent servants
circling and doing tasks.

The glass becomes so shiny
and it really does delight us
for I always leave a tip
for the working *window vipers*.

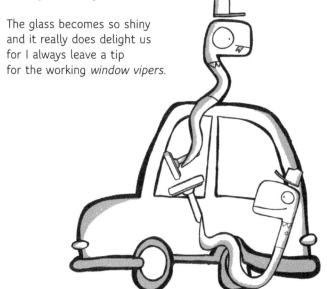

64. Silly Sally Salamander?

Was Sally Salamander a silly salamander?
her family were stricter
than some military commanders

they demanded she behave and she stop being silly
on tropical days they still acted very chilly.

Sally Salamander loved Billy Salamander
but his father was a bully
who would bully salamanders

the father said to Billy *"Billy I think you are silly"*
take responsibility and do not fall for Sally".

Billy Salamander loved Sally Salamander
they weren't that alike like a salmon and a panda

but opposites attract plus they both loved to rap
so they hip hopped from home
to run away no looking back.

So Sally Salamander and Billy Salamander
spilled out laughter and happy ever afters

they lived on a hill beneath starlit skies
they were sparks in their hearts
and fires in their eyes.

65. Snail Tales

A snail knight wears snail mail
a snail cup is a snail grail
snail hammers need snail nails
and snail stories are snail tales.

A snail school is snail Yale
a snail prison, snail jail
when a snail sells, that's snail sales
and snail stories are snail tales.

Snail post is snail mail
snail spinach is snail kale
snail beer is snail ale
and snail stories are snail tales.

A snail bloke is a snail male
snail trains run on snail rails
a snail cry is a snail wail
and snail stories are snail tales.

Snail weddings have snail veils
snail journeys are snail trails
snail ships have snail sails
and snail stories are snail tales.

Snail wins or snail fails
snail sun or snail hail
snails strong until snails frail
snail stories are snail tales.

66. Tortoise on Tour

I'll go around the world,
I'm a tortoise on *touuuuuuuur*
I'm a tourist and a tortoise
and I'll *touuuuuuuu*r even more
than a tourist who's toured since before I was born
I'm a tortoise, I'm a tortoise,
I'm a tortoise on *touuuuuuuur*

I'll go to Togo, then Turkey, then Tonga
then Trinidad and Tobago, then I will stay longer
in Thailand, Tuvalu and then Timbuktu
I'm a tortoise on *touuuuuuuur*
to explore somewhere new

I'll take my camera and I'll get to snapping
I'll take my bags once I've finished packing
I'll take myself, a touring tortoise with style
but leaving my town is still taking a *whiiiiiiiiiiiiiile...*

67. Stock Market Croc

Croco worked on the telephone
he had to make calls snappy
making all these quick decisions
kept his strict boss happy.

Croco spoke on the telephone
he always talked so snappy
his boss was such a grumpy wolf
all growly, howly, yappy.

Though Croco worked so rapidly
his wolf boss never smiled
all he did was yell at Croco
Yelling *"dial, Croco dial!!"*

68. Isaac Knewton

Isaac was a newt, who knew tons of things
so Isaac Knewton was the name that he earned,
he knew tons about ponds
he knew tons about swamps
and he thought about the way the world turned.

Isaac was a newt, who knew tons of things
so Isaac Knewton was the name he was called,
he knew tons about logs
tadpoles and frogs
and he thought about what makes things fall.

Isaac was a newt, who knew tons of things
he was the best scientist around,
he saw an apple in a tree
and then discovered gravity
yeah, Isaac really held it down.

69. Camille Chameleon

Camille Camille Chameleon
always did her thing
that's just how she lived her life
being comfortable in her skin.

The forest was a mix of colour
but mainly shades of green
so Camille wore shocking pink,
the difference was extreme.

"Be careful" many others said.
*"Are you sure that that's allowed
have you heard of a chameleon
that stands out from the crowd?"*

Camille wasn't cautious though
she wasn't afraid of trouble
if anyone tried to halve her shine
she'd make sure that it doubled.

In time the fear that others had
just grew into amazement
Camille taught the forest
not to camouflage their greatness

Camille Camille Chameleon
always did her thing
she said *"why should we live our life
by always blending in?"*

70. Acro-Bat

Flipping.
    Twirling.
Dipping.
   Curling.
Twisting.
  Turning.

 Swishing.
  Swirling.
Swooping.
   Diving.
    Swooshing.

Flying.

I can do all that with my eyes closed...

cos I'm an... ***ACRO-BAT.***

71. Centipede Centre-Back

Christine was a Centipede
did she have a hundred legs?
Technically that is not true
she's got thirty instead.

But thirty's plenty for her job
shall I tell you what she does?
she's a centre-back on a football team
and Christine's very good

she'll tackle any striker
her legs will bring them down
and even though she's a centipede
she never goes to ground.

Fifteen left feet and fifteen right
she's skilful on the ball
diving headers are her thing
'cos Christine's not that tall

but still there is a problem here
and please let me explain
it takes so long to put on her boots
that she always misses the game!

72. Yo! Bumblebee

Yo! Bumblebee don't be a humble bee
you work really hard and never grumble bee.
Yo! Bumblebee don't be a grumble bee
you hum through the air and never tumble bee.

Yo! Bumblebee don't be a tumble bee
when you land on the plant you never stumble bee.
Yo! bumblebee don't be a stumble bee
when you get into the nectar, never fumble bee.

Yo! Bumblebee don't be a fumble bee
you know where to go, and never bumble bee.
No! bumblebee don't be a bumble bee
with neat honey that's never in a jumble bee.

Oh! Bumblebee, I'm in a jumble, bee
I just made a blueberry crumble, bee
my tummy is starting up a rumble, bee
could I borrow some honey from a humble bee?

Yo! Bumblebee! I won't mumble bee
you're the best bee a bee could become you bee!
Go Bumblebee! Go! Bumblebee!
Bring that fuzzy fizzy buzzy busy buzz to me.

73. Caterpillar Rapper Killer

I'm a caterpillar
rapper killer
thriller on the mic

I'm a caterpillar
rapper killer
not vanilla right?

I'm a caterpillar
rapper killer
spill a couple rhymes

I'm a caterpillar
rapper killer
iller with my lines...

I'm the griller
of gorillas
if they step into my room

caterpillar
floor filler
I got all the hottest tunes

before I fall asleep
I'll make the bass
go **BOOM!**

I hope I never change
when I come out
of this cocoon...

74. I'm a Celebrity

I'm not terrified of tarantulas
tap dancing on my toes
you could televise them tickle me
on tele I suppose.

I'm not terrified of tarantulas
teeming down my top
you could even stream it
I'd go viral on TikTok

I'm not terrified of tarantulas
tap dancing on my toes
truly it's my talent
can you throw me on a show?

I'm not terrified of tarantulas
they don't tempt me towards terror
but if you didn't film it
that's a terrible error.

I'm not terrified of tarantulas
tap dancing on my toes
it's terribly tantalizing
to be well known don't you know?

I'm not terrified of tarantulas
they don't shake me to my core
what truly terrifies me
is not being famous any more.

75. Fight or Flight?

If I have to fight a creature
and that creature's smaller than me

then I will teach a lesson
and I'll be home before tea

I will stand my ground
there's no one on their grind like me

I will crack my knuckles
and then I will my grind my teeth.

If I have to fight a creature
and that creature's smaller than me

then you had best believe
that I'm as brave as brave can be

my opponent is so tiny
I'll need a microscope to seek

can someone get a microscope
and can you bring it me?

Somebody got a microscope
my opponent I can see...

Wait... what is that!? call off the fight!
I really need to

FLEAAAAAAAAAAAA

76. Mantras

If you're looking for some answers
I get deeper than Atlantis

if you wanna take me on
I don't really like your chances

if I have to then I'll flick you
kick you somewhere near where France is

my mind is very practiced
and my hind legs spring in backflips.

I am smarter, I am sharper
then the sharpest bit of antlers

I am larger than an ant is
and I know karate dances

you can find me in the dojo
where I meditate with mantras

that is my holy temple
for I am a praying Mantis.

77. The Nonsense Wasp

Compare me to Muhammad Ali
I float like a butterfly
sting like a... Wasp.

Oh my, oh my
that didn't rhyme
I don't have to do it all of the... Hours.

Did it again.
that's not nice,
ouch that was cold
as cold as... Showers.

I rhymed showers and hours
so gimme my flowers
pay me some dough
like I'm rolling out flour!

Now we're getting ahead
call me the baker
I like baking... Muffins.

Stuffing these words
into all of these lines
they sting like a wasp
when there's sugar to find

I'll make it sound good
most of the time

But the thing about poems
they don't have to... Make sense.

78. Shrug

I'm snug as a bug in a rug.
No, I'm snug as a slug in a jug.
No, I'm snug as a bug and a slug
in a jug on the rug.

No, I'm snug as a bug and a slug in a mug
in a jug on the rug.
No, I'm snug as a bug and a slug
and a thug in a hug in a mug in a jug on the rug.

No, I'm snug as a bug and a... okay I'll stop.

Just joking.

I'm snug as a bug and a slug and a thug
in a hug who have dug in a plug
in a mug in a jug on the rug.
No, I'm snug as a bug and a slug and a...
Okay I'll stop for real.

Joking!

I'm snug as a bug and a slug
and a thug and a pug in a hug
who have dug in a plug and they glug in a mug
in a jug on the rug.

No, I'm snug as a bug and a slug in some Ugg's
and a... okay fine, you win.
(Shrug).

79. Sunday Morning

It's Sunday morning, I don't wanna get up
I don't wanna do any chores
Dad's trying to get the hoover out
and Mum's knocking on my door

they hover around like hoverflies
always buzzing at me,
"come on get up you lazy thing
There's things to do you see!"

I wish I was an insect
the size of a tiny stick
then I could hide so easily
and that would do the trick.

It's Sunday morning, I'm so tired
but what can I do? I shrug
if I could be born again
then I'd come back as a bed bug.

80. My Grandma's Hairy Ears

My Grandma has hairy ears
little, wiry tufts that sprout
maybe that's why he can't hear
and we always have to shout

my Grandma has hairy ears
little cactus-spines of white
even when I stand so near
she just says *"what!?"* all night.

My Grandma has hairy ears
she reminds me of a yeti
it's been growing all these years
into strands of grey spaghetti.

One day my Grandad had enough
he gave her ears a trim
but the hair grew back like straightaway
did she play a trick on him?

I said Grandma, *"how did you do that?
with that hair like a spindly twig?"*
she said, *"I don't like all your chat
so I've made myself an EAR WIG!"*

81. Cricket

Christopher Cricket
was into his sport
he'd wear his whites
then walk onto the lawn

Christopher Cricket
loved the sound of the crowd
he heard nothing but crickets
from around the ground

Christopher Cricket
stood on the green
the grass was neat
twelve trainers gleamed

he stretched six legs
flexed three bodies
oh Chris was a pro
this wasn't a hobby

he'd hit the ball hard
he'd hit the ball fast
he'd watch the ball spin
then skim on the grass

he knew where to hit the ball
he knew where to stick it
you guessed it, Chris
was terrific at...
tennis.
.

82. Fruit Bat

I am a Fruit Bat, yeah, a fruit bat
do you really, really, know what fruit is?

I'm talking apples, I'm talking cherries
I'm talking papaya, I'm talking strawberries
I'm talking pineapples and apricots
I'm talking kiwis and coconuts

I'm talking oranges and nectarines
I'm talking pomegranates and the freshest peach
I'm talking bananas, I'm talking mangos
I'm talking pears and avocados

I'm talking limes, I'm talking lemons
grapes, raspberries, blueberries, melons.

I am a Fruit Bat, yeah, a fruit bat
do you know what my favourite food is?

I am a Fruit Bat, yeah, a fruit bat
It's... *Spaghetti Bolognaise.*

83. Webster's Words

There's so much to see on the spider web
it takes up all my time
reading all of the spider threads
that my friends post online.

There's so much spin on the spider web
I'm not sure what to do
"I bit Peter Parker" some spider said
I'm not sure if that's true.

I try to use my Spidey sense
to work out fact from fiction
but me and all my spider friends
might have a web addiction.

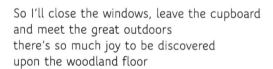

I need a change, to turn the page
I can't waste away inside
when my dad was around this age
he was out catching flies...

So I'll close the windows, leave the cupboard
and meet the great outdoors
there's so much joy to be discovered
upon the woodland floor

I'll play football with a team of voles
I'll kick with all eight legs
you will see the dreamy goal
WHEN I HIT THE BACK OF THE NET!

84. Heads or Tails

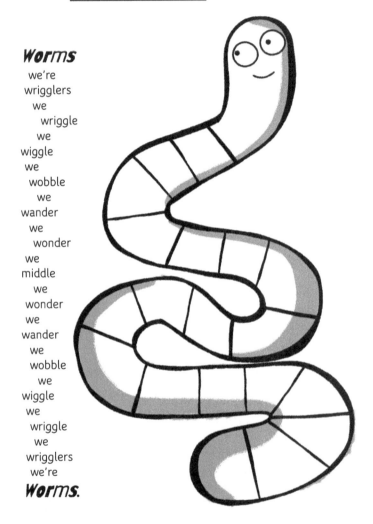

Worms
we're
wrigglers
we
 wriggle
we
wiggle
we
 wobble
 we
wander
 we
 wonder
we
middle
 we
 wonder
we
wander
 we
 wobble
 we
wiggle
we
 wriggle
 we
wrigglers
 we're
Worms.

85. Emily Anemone

I'll bet you any money
I can really say anemone
it's hard to say anemone
it's sort of like an enemy

I'll bet the money anyway
and try to say anemone
but what if the anemone
is also called Emma?

Then its Emma the anemone
or what if she was Emily?
Is Emily anemone in anyway an enemy?
An enemy anemone, HELP!

86. Jellyfish

If a jellyfish was smelly
would it then be called a smelly-fish?
And if it had a telly
would it then be called a telly-fish?
But how d'you tell a smelly-fish
apart from any telly-fish
and how do they look different
from any regular jellyfish?

If a jellyfish wore wellies
would it then be called a welly-fish?
and if it started raining
would it ask for an umbrelly-fish?
But how d'you tell a welly-fish
apart from an umbrelly-fish
aside from every telly-fish
and also all the smelly-fish?

If Jellyfish had bellies
would they then be called a belly-fish?
And if they had a belly
would they fill it with a jelly dish?
But if you feed a jelly dish
to any telly-smelly-fish
then you might cause some jealousy
from the umbrelly-welly-fish...

So are they then a jelly-fish
'cos they can't eat a jelly dish?
but if they ate a jelly dish
they'd turn back to a jellyfish?

87. Krill Bill

Bill was a krill, a cool chill Krill
if a krill could be chill, it was Bill

he made them bills, so Bill was chill
if a krill had a skill, it was Bill

'cos Bill had skills, his skills were ill
if a krill knew the drill, it was Bill

Bill was a thrill, he let lyrics spill
if a krill could rhyme brill, it was Bill

he'd flow from Seville to the coast of Brazil
if a krill wasn't still, it was Bill

Bill did as he willed, heated mics like grills
if a krill earned a mill, it was Bill

Bill had to be good, the rap world is tough
out there it is krill or be krilled.

88. Mobster Lobster

Mobster Lobster

he lost the plot.
Does he care? He does not.

Mobster Lobster

he wants his money
His only soft spot is his tummy.

He likes good food, expensive taste
he smokes cigars, he drinks champagne.

Mobster Lobster

he does crime so well.
He hides his earnings, using shells.

Mobster Lobster

he made a lot
'til he got lobbed in a lobster pot.

89. <u>Barry</u>

Barry Cuda cruises near Cuba
so be careful where you choose to scuba

Barry Cuda has a needle-nose
like a compass it points where he needs to go

Barry Cuda has an evil grin
silver scales and the sleekest fins

Barry Cuda has a cunning look
he's way too clever for the fishing hooks

Barry Cuda has crunching jaws
for lunch he'll munch on swimmer's shorts

and if he's hungry, did you know?
He'll nibble on fingers and scavenge your toes

if you lend him an ear, you won't get it back
maybe your nose is a midnight snack?

All this worry I really do carry
that's why I'll never swim near Barry!

90. Gotta Eat

We're the cleverest in the sea
we speak six different languages
we hunt in packs and lunch is packed
with fish finger sandwiches

our teeth are dagger-sharp
our eyes are full of cunning
our fins slice through the water
plus our tails are stunning

we can be silent stalkers
or loud talkers making waves
technically, we're Orcas
but the way that we behave

means they call us names
they call us killer whales
like we are just murderers
who should be still in jail.

But is that fair? Is that right?
it's not polite at least
we're just acting naturally
does that make us feasting beasts?

They call us killer whales
and that really makes us grumpy
trembling penguins seal your lips
because it's not our fault we're hungry!

91. Golfin' Dolphin

92. Skate Fish

Swim... and... push... and... coast...
That's the way she flowed
just a rebel in the sea
with no place to go.

It all started when she was six
didn't know any tricks
just a young skate fish
trying to get in the mix

made her own skateboard
from driftwood on the floor
decorated it all
with seashells from the shore.

She stayed on her grind
could kick flip in no time
focusing her mind
splashing down the half pipe.

She never felt more free
skating shallow or deep
then the Olympic team
said *"please represent the sea?"*

Swim... and... push... and... coast...
That's the way she flowed
just a rebel with a dream
now she's going for gold.

93. Dragonfish?

I'm just like a dragon, I'm just like a dragon
I'm even covered in scales

I'm just like a dragon, I'm just like a dragon
check out my spiky tail

I'm just like a dragon, I'm just like a dragon
see my sharp-tooth grin

I'm just like a dragon, I'm just like a dragon
my fins fan
        out like wings

I'm quite like a dragon, *a bit* like a dragon
there's just one issue for me.

It's hard to be a dragon, *exactly* like a dragon
'cos I can't breathe fire in the sea!

94. Crab Driver

I'm a crab driver, I'll take you to the sea
hop up on my back and don't forget to pay me

I'm a crab driver, I'll collect you from the shore
when the beach gets busy, it'll cost you more

it's my honourable job to provide a safe trip
and if you feel like it, you can give me a tip.

You can talk if you want, I can talk really well
I'm not a shy crab driver, I really come out my shell

so fasten your seatbelts and we'll head to the tide
as I move side to side and side to side

I only travel sideways, wherever we go toward
enjoy your journey but it won't be straightforward.

95. Magician

Crusty Crustacean had a mission
but everyone doubted his decision

he didn't pull rabbits out of hats
or shuffle 52 cards in packs

he didn't wear a flowing cape
or make daring quick escapes

he couldn't vanish into thin air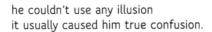
or twist balloons into a bear

he couldn't use any illusion
it usually caused him true confusion.

But Crusty Crustacean had a mission
he'd show the rockpool he was a *magician!*

One day his show would be slick and neat
every magic trick could be a magic treat

one day he'd turn barnacles into confetti
and green seaweed to blue spaghetti

but before that, magic could still be seen
the true magic of how he followed his dream

if you ever see him, the magic will grab ya
Crusty spelling out..

CRABRA-KEDABRA!

96. Narwhals and Needles

Narwhals are known for a tusk
on their head
it's shaped just like a sword.

Narwhals are known
for this tusk on their head
but do you know what it's really for?

It's not for fighting
or a quill for writing
or to hang up a satellite dish.

Narwhals are known for a tusk
on their head
but do you know what it really is?

When you know like I do
it might surprise you
the answer does not seem fitting

it's not a tusk
no it's a needle
that the narwhals need for knitting.

They knit all night
beside the ice
but what do they do when its finished?

At an iceberg shop
they sell their stock
of warm winter hats and mittens.

97. <u>Ol Oyster</u>

●l Oyster
why are you shy?

●ll Oyster?
Why do you have so many eyes?

●llll Oyster
do you watch the fish swim by?

●llllllll Oyster
if a crab comes do you hide?

●llllllllllllll Oyster
can you feel the currents twirl?

●llllllllllllllllllllllllllll Oyster
can you see the coral curl?

●lllllllllllllllllllllllllllllllllllllllllllllllllll Oyster
can you teach us about your world?

●llllllllllllllllllllllllllllllllllllllllllllllllllllllllllllllllllllllllllllllllllllllllllllllll Oyster
how do you turn grit into a pearl?

98. Shark in the Park

Hark, there's a shark
in a park in the dark
did it park up an Ark
made of bark in the park?
A shark in an Ark
that would park in the dark
in a park for a lark
is a shark we should mark.

99. A Space in the Sea

I want to be a comet cod
I'd like to be a planet plaice
a Milky Way manta ray
orbiting the deepest space

I want to be a cosmic crab
a supernova seahorse too
Saturn pattern on my scales
racing rings around all you

a jellyfish from Jupiter
a narwhal from Neptune
a minky whale from Mercury
with eyes like two bright moons

I want to rocket round a reef
somewhere out where Mars is
but if I can't be any of that...

At least I am a starfish

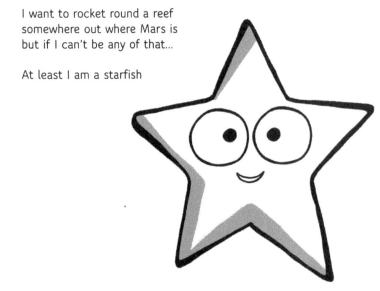

100. **Dear Humanity**

Dear Humanity,

I'm the gentlest on the planet, that is a reality
no I didn't plan it, it just happened naturally
I surf on a wave and behave kinda casually
a dipper with my flippers
that I dip until they paddle me.

Underwater plants, yeah that's how I put on calories
I eat so many of them that they actually fatten me
I swim kinda slow,
like there's nowhere that I have to be
not a single animal eats or chases after me.

Still that doesn't mean there is never a catastrophe
there is one animal that brings about disaster, see
you ride around on boats,
and you showboats damage me
this letter says do better.

Yours Sincerely,

Hugh (Manatee)

101. I Used to Know an Ocean

I had a friend called Coral
but I've not seen her in ages
she disappeared quite gradually
we lost our touch in stages

I used to know some Orca kids
oh they made quite the splash
until they both got kidnapped
to make somebody some cash

so now in little pens
they're forced to swim around
their bodies write a message
and their fins curve into frowns

I used to know a turtle
and she planned to circle seas
but she got caught in plastic
and it made it hard to breathe

I feel things very deeply
I guess that's why I sing
and swim deeper than I used to
to escape you shallow things

I used to know an ocean
who told me soothing tales
now her story's saddening.
And I too, am a *blue* whale.

ABOUT THE AUTHOR

Christian Foley is a rapper, writer and a teacher... all at once. This is his debut poetry book! Him and Rob have also written two picture books called "The Oddsocktopus" and "Some Bears".

It took Christian three years to write all these poems. But he was doing other stuff in between... like trying to rhyme with "purple-orange". He got as far as "turtle porridge". Does that work?

ABOUT THE ILLUSTRATOR

Rob Turner is an illustrator, animator and teacher... all at once. Him and Christian work at the same school! This is Rob and Christian's third book together. Rob spent a lot of time on these 101 illustrations. It's not easy to draw a rapping caterpillar you know.

For each of the chapter titles, Rob thought it would be funny to draw Christian getting crushed by an elephant, stuck in a cobweb, or about to be squeezed by a snake. They remain good friends. Stay tuned for what they do next!

ALSO BY CHRISTIAN FOLEY & ROB TURNER

THE ODDSOCKTOPUS
(Ages 5-7)

"Christian Foley's rhyme swirl and whirl, they twirl and curl through this underwater world. Dancing words twist and turn to the rhythm of the sea. This is storytelling with a Hip-Hop spin. Dive in deep. Journey with an octopus who has eight new socks, and a very odd tale to tell"

- Michael Rosen

SOME BEARS
(Ages 0-5)

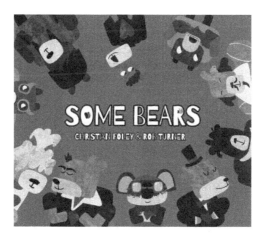

Sometimes we all feel lost / we can barely find our way /

here's a book to get your bearings / will you open up today?

"Some Bears" is a book that helps children when dealing with feelings. Whatever our lives reveal, there is always the chance to heal.

I'M TREMBLING PENGUIN. THESE FELLAS SURE **DO** HAVE SOME COLD SKILLS. WHAT WAS YOUR FAVOURITE POEM? MINE WAS KRILL BILL (HE'S PRETTY CHILL).

I HATED POEM NUMBER 90. CAN YOU GUESS WHY!? AND WHAT WAS UP WITH **GOLFIN' DOLPHIN? DID** THEY FORGET THE WORDS... WHO KNOWS... IT'S IMPOSSIBLE TO GUESS WHAT THOSE GUYS WERE THINKING... MAYBE WE'LL FIND OUT NEXT TIME!!! UNTIL THEN... KEEP UP WITH THE BABBLIN' ANIMAL RAPS.. **OR** AS I CALL THEM... BARS!!